ANOTHER SPRING

Robin Matthews

ANOTHER SPRING

collected poems

Worldwind Books   Albuquerque

Printed in the United States of America
First Printing, 2014
ISBN: 978-0-938513-50-6
Library of Congress Control Number: 2014946395

Acknowledgments
  The following were published under the name William J. Matthews: "Dusk on 5th Street" appeared in the Winter 1968 issue of *Epos*. "Reverie" (as "Lilac Reverie") and "Eternity" appeared in Vol. 1, No. 1 of *Sanskaras*. "On the Eve of Nixon" appeared as "Poem in Lieu of an Editorial" in Vol. 1, No. 2 of *Sanskaras*. "Refuge", "Fire in the Hole!", and "March" appeared in Vol. 1, No. 3 of *Sanskaras*. "Dupont Circle/Everywhere" and "night walk in the holy land" appeared in Vol. 1, No. 4 of *Sanskaras*.
  Photos pages 19 and 47 courtesy Christopher Barr; photos page 31 and cover (Sandia Mountains) courtesy Zelda Gatuskin; photos pages 2, 11, 28, 32, 39, 60, 79, 116 and cover (Virginia Lane) courtesy Robin Matthews.
  Cover design by Ashley N. Jordan; cover photo montage by Zelda Gatuskin and Ashley N. Jordan; cover background photo (bee and flower) by M. Ruby Nelson.

WORLDWIND BOOKS
an imprint of
Amador Publishers, LLC
Albuquerque, New Mexico
www.amadorbooks.com

ANOTHER SPRING
Contents

Photographs

*For my daughters, Raven Alita and Kiowa Taos,
and my granddaughters, Sagesse Eva and Teagan Erin.*

Easter morning

In the woods from my back deck
the soft emerging green of hickories and oaks,
poplars and maples, sweet gums and sourwoods,
is seasoned with the white of dogwoods and wild plum;

the beeches have thrust off
the shrivelled leaves of last fall
and at the tip of each branch
a needle-like brown tip
waits to any moment open
into green leaves.

the redbuds line the roads with magenta;
tulips are fading, azaleas about to begin,
lilacs are intense,
ferns unfurling once again
their ancient fronds;

hummingbirds are back,
male goldfinches have turned bright yellow,
wrens serenade each other
from fifty yards apart.

there are bees about,
not nearly as many as there used to be,
but I am glad to see any bees,
and today I saw the first butterflies;

amidst ascendant spring
it is hard to credit the remembered
snow and cold rain of winter.

on the front lawn my protected invasives
and ornamentals are thriving:

the weeping willow I planted a few years ago
is now a substantial tree;
the pink dogwood for the first time
is covered with blooms;

the Japanese maple has become a very small but perfect tree:
they grow so very slow,
I wonder how tall I shall see it get.
I am already past threescore and ten,
but well shy of fourscore;
I feel healthy and fit enough,
my doctor tells me that she
would take me for much younger
if she had not my chart before her;
and we do live long these days.

I might be still going strong at 93 like
a farmer I met in Vermont
who owned a mountain and a valley,
and seemed still full of life.
But that was long ago;
he is surely gone now.

There are much younger friends,
gone these many years,
with whom I would expect to be still conversing.
We have no fixed term.

But every spring implies
another spring.

Charlotte County, Virginia
20 April 2014

virginia winter

mostly rain
is how i think of winter in virginia
i love the sound of it
sometimes a gentle pattering on the metal roof
other times a torrent

a few years ago for several
there was hardly any rain
winter or summer
which was hard;
in summer even trees wilted
and we worried about our wells

but winter seems to be back to rain
in the mountains to the west
and in the north of the state
there has been snow this year
but hereabouts only rain
it's raining now,
it rained this morning, with a little ice,
it will rain tonight
it will rain tomorrow

sometimes there is quite a lot of snow
which is pretty and very quiet,
no patter involved with snow
but quickly it melts,
frequently redefines as rain and washes all away
and then there is rain again

if it is raining when i wake
i will turn over and slide gently into sleep again
i love to sleep with the patter of the rain
upon the roof

sleep,
sleep,
gentle, gentle sleep,
soft as the patter of rain upon the roof

Charlotte County, Virginia
10 January 2014

nascent spring

the trees are greening now,
just in the last two days there has been this big change.

the maple branches have been red-tipped for weeks.
there is a maple that grows here
that is peculiar for producing its seeds
long before the leaves.
the seeds in those strange vessels that we called helicopters
when such things were new
(we call that childhood)

the beeches have held all winter
last summer's dessicated leaves
but now shed them, pushed off by the new shoots.
there are many beeches in my thirty acres of wood,
but they are small. eventually
it will be a beechwood forest, if it is not cleared.
i hope they will live to be large.
i would like to see that, but i am not likely to live that long.
beeches grow slow.

it is fine enough now. lots of cedar, some pine,
native short-needled pine, not loblollies;
now overtaking those are poplars and sweet gums and maples,
the occasional sourwood,
lots of wild privet that has naturalised itself all over my acres,
a few hemlocks — a surprise, those —
wild azaleas, holly;

almost defeated now the alien kudzu, a harsh battle
also the poison ivy that was strangling the trees.
(i know, it's a native, i should love it, but i do not.)

today outside the kitchen window
i saw a really big black snake, at least three feet i am sure.
a squirrel was fascinated.
he got amazingly close, watching it wriggle its way past.
i wondered if he would survive his curiosity.
he did.
the black snake kept going to wherever it was headed.
probably to eat some field mice, or maybe a juicy chipmunk.
early yet for birds' eggs
squirrels might not easily submit
to being squeezed to death.
i suppose the snake is too cautious to attempt a squirrel
they are so
active.

then on the porch, much later
i watched two squirrels, obviously babies.
seems early, but maybe squirrels do that.
they were chasing each other all over the princess tree.
this is an odd tree.
where most trees have pith it has empty space.
the woodpeckers have made many large holes in the trunk,
seeking insect tidbits no doubt.
the squirrels enter a hole and come out another
way down or up the tree.

tonight there will be storms that are in tennessee now.
then it will be cooler again, for awhile.

all these things are happening.
and i watch.
it is not so bad.

Charlotte County, Virginia
11 April 2013

return to virginia

everything lush this year,
so much rain,
too much for the farmers no doubt,
but i like it well
compared to the dry of recent years.

green patched with brown,
wind moving like waves through wheat fields
alongside rows of fire-cured tobacco,
and over all
the raucous music of crows

Charlotte County, Virginia
summer 2013

end of april

brown march is now a memory,
the woods are thick with green.
beside the house azaleas are blooming,
undulant with butterflies and bumblebees.

i saw the pesky groundhog today
who loves to tunnel under my house
and in the woods a deer
was startled by my morning walk
and startled me in turn.

the feeders are laden with
cardinals and goldfinches
chickadees and wrens
chipping sparrows
purple finches and nuthatches
on the ground beneath
doves and squirrels
feast upon the overflow.

the woodpecker who was a winter regular
is no more, perhaps preferring
fresh insects to old sunflower seeds.

i have not seen a hummingbird
though my neighbour tells me
they have arrived,
and not yet heard a whippoorwill,
but the mornings are raucous with jays.

nights are cold lately,
even the days cool enough for a jacket
except in the sun.
it is easy weather to bask in,
forgetting how,
just beyond,
summer's heat stalks us,
soon to pounce.

Charlotte County, Virginia
26 April 2013

passage

sun is on the far horizon
shadows deepen beneath the trees
breezes quicken
crows chatter

night falls
the woods become
secret

whippoorwills emerge
from the undergrowth
to utter their strange cry

frogs bestir and croak
coyotes howl

moon presents itself
transition is complete

Charlotte County, Virginia
24 May 2013

one robin

how unusual,
you don't normally see one robin
but big clusters of them
and there was one robin yesterday as well

the same one i wonder?

a cardinal came swooping
across the lawn and landed
almost atop the lone robin.
surprise was the reaction.
and then the robin circled, on the ground,
then flew away.

i wonder what that was all about.
we do not really know what any of it is about
who sit here thinking we are atop the pyramid
and really know nothing.

Charlotte County, Virginia
10 May 2013

old now

not such a surprise.
coming for a long time.
the not so tight skin, the colder cold.

waking now to so many alternate realities.
the might have beens

the paths abandoned
the paths overlooked
the never tried
and of course the once taken
there taking

the south valley.
lama.
canada.

now suddenly the unexpected
stoking of such old fires.
poetry reawakened by prose
surging again in the abandoned circuits
so long without electricity,

well,
not to question
but only
enjoy.

Charlotte County, Virginia
19 February 2013

boyhood revisited

maples,
silver & green,
yellow, red,
bare,
masquerading as campfire.

cedar water,
cold,
but irresistible,
astringent as canvas-filtered dawn.

shoulders & backs aching deliciously of canoes,
we moved,
mysterious as water,
into & out
of summer,

exploring ourselves along the oswego & the maurice,
the great egg harbor,
unlearning concrete & steel,
learning cold, hot,
experimenting with naked,

troubled always
by the restless images

above the shattered surface of our pool.

sometime in the '60s
revisited 9 March 2014

paused

sitting on the edge of a mountain
watching the eagles in the summer of 1970
the sangre de cristo rose
cathedral-like
from the desert.

irene
was probably in our orange tent
half a mile away,
the only one on earth
who knew where i was.
the vw was miles away
down the mountain path
that traced the brook
that everyone called the river.

where could i be today
so easily so far from connexions
wanted or not?
without laptop, iphone, facebook,
with no google earth,
without even radio or cell phone.

not disconnected,
but unconnected

except to the soaring eagles,
the mountains and the desert,
paused on the brink
in the summer of 1970.

Charlotte County, Virginia
9 June 2013

anamnesis

remembering
driving home from jemez,
forty years ago

the highway bends tight away
from jemez springs;
sky glitters gold above green and red;

below san ysidro
the front end of the vw
sways from side to side,
floating, trembling against the wind
that sweeps from the desert;

the day reddens and burns itself out,
and albuquerque shimmers
in a great pit of dark.

Charlotte County, Virginia
14 June 2013

Gazing at an Old Photo

These five figures sitting, knees bent, on the narrow lip
that served as a balcony to our makeshift,
funky apartment in the South Valley
have come storming out of the past and overwhelmed me.

All gone.
Forty plus years separate me from this photo,
only my then infant daughter remains easily findable,
now older than I was then.

I look so apart from the others, sitting gazing forward;
I *was* a bit apart, always observing, never quite engaged;
I am still.

Christina with her enigmatic half-smile,
how I would love to walk into this scene and meet her again.
But, ah, do I wish to meet her as she is now and as I am now,
or as she was then and I was then?

Christopher, the photographer,
who memory tells me has only moments before
set up the camera
and assumed his position alongside Christina,
deceptively casual with either cigarette or joint in hand.

Finally Irene and Raven, in front of our makeshift screen door;
beloved Irene,
now so unbelievably and utterly alienated from me for so long.
If I could revisit that moment I would hold her close
with an intensity that would puzzle her.

On her lap sweet baby Raven,
her tiny hands folded in her mother's.

None could have guessed that only Raven and I
would travel down the years together.

The shutter clicked, and here we are,
we five,
preserved as a moment in time.

Charlotte County, Virginia
15 February 2014

Photo courtesy of Christopher Barr. In the South Valley, late summer of 1971. Left to right: the author, Christina, Christopher, Irene holding baby Raven. Raven is the daughter of the author and Irene.

Poem to My Father

After all these years,
old enough myself that I am a grandfather,
finally I am ready to call you Dad.
So many years I put you out of my mind
as though you never existed,
angry at you for being not there
for all the years of my growing up.

How unfair,
for surely you did not walk into the sea
expecting never to emerge alive,
leaving on the beach a widowed mother,
a two-year old son,
a mortgage, a car your widow could not drive.

She mastered driving. She found work as a seamstress,
we moved back home, her mother and sister moved in
and then, when the War ended,
her sister's children and husband.
Mom was resourceful, she managed.
God, I hardly realised how much it took,
but she managed.

Earlier in that dreadful day
I am sure you played with me
at the edge of the surf.
Everyone always told me how much you loved me,
how you'd walk around our suburban neighbourhood
carrying me with you, showing me off
in the brief time we had together.

You loved the sea —
there are all those black and white photos
of you and Mom on the beach —
and I am sure you were teaching me
to love the sea as well,
to be unafraid.

The seed fell on fertile soil, I always loved the ocean.
I terrorised my mother and your family
by how much I loved the the sea.
To their credit they did not try to keep me from it.
Yet I cannot remember you at all.
My memories begin shortly after, at Grandma's house
— your mother — where Mom and I took
immediate, temporary refuge.

I wish I could remember playing
that day in the surf with you
I would like so much to remember you.
And even more to have grown up knowing you.

Charlotte County, Virginia
4 January 2014

pivot

the sun is shining.
there are clouds, but not many.
for a while they banked
dark grey with vague foreboding
on the western edge,
but nothing came of it.

the air is temperate,
the lawn a patchwork
of sunlight and shade.
the breeze rises and falls
fitfully
soughing through the trees.

a day that seems
to explain life
without the need for words.

Charlotte County, Virginia
10 May 2013

thunder poem

thunderous as weather
shaking
thin virginia clapboards
unreliable as spring warmth
tropical or arctic
with fitful embrace
bermuda high
canadian low
my mood
does alter itself
to fit
the sudden motion
of internal pressures
external resistances
and all is
contingent

Charlotte County, Virginia
1997

evolution

snow falls on empty plains
waves scour lifeless continents

in rockface crevice lichens grow
to become in far when

frantic and carnivorous
at last human

ultimately flawed

Charlotte County, Virginia
1997

Virginia redux

rain
on tin roof
rushing
pounding,
hissing
of space heater,
brittle rustle of
plastic shower curtain
attempting
to be door:
winter in virginia

Charlotte County, Virginia
1997

25

August

There is a storm breeding out there perhaps —
it is far from the first of this strange august
but the weather is strange everywhere now
so that one wonders if ever in our life
it will again fall into an easy pattern.

usually, i think not,
i think rather that it will become
stranger & stranger so that even here
in virginia we will plant tomatoes
in july and pray it does not freeze
before september & another year we will
be harvesting them through november.

i would be not awfully surprised
if it snowed next week. if it rained
for a month or the sky cleared
and burned merciless until christmas
it would be only hard to bear,
but no longer surprising

it surprises me mostly that we
are so lucky
while less fortunate countries
blister or drown for our technological misjudgments

it seems now already the storm has
changed its mind & passed on,
the trees have quietened,
only the persistent pattern of
the insect night remains.

Charlotte County, Virginia
August 1977

confession

all right.
the fire burns,
adds its burden of smoke
to the rain heavy
virginia air

summer in here
is an illusion
sustained by hickory & beech logs
sheltering us among
lemon trees
and avocado
philodendron and
cacti, jade plants, swedish ivy
outside is winter's
cold, winter's wet.

it should be enough,
i want it to be enough.

but in fact i'd give a lot
for a drink of good whiskey tonight.
i'd like to be on the corner
of 7th ave. & bleeker with a week's pay in my wallet.

Charlotte County, Virginia
January 1976

The author in southside Virginia, summer of 1976, with his wife, Jane, and daughters, Kiowa and Raven.

bugga lump

oh you bloody machine
how i hate you
go on churn it out
bugga lump bugga lump
bugga lump bugga lump
ten thousand copies in green
ten thousand copies in black
bugga lump bugga lump

oh for money the things they make us do
ten years minding machines
nine then and one now
skilled craftsman: set the ink set the water
bugga lump multilith bugga lump

questionnaires for employees
forms to keep records of forms
more tracts for jesus freaks
more publicity for the march of dimes
bugga lump bugga lump
at least bugga lump now provides
money to keep my land safe
so with boredom thirty-six hours a week
i subsidise the rest

bugga lump bugga lump
two more days and then some *my* time
three days to use body and mind
steel myself for more bugga lump
bugga lump bugga lump
bugga lump bugga lump

Lynchburg, Virginia
1974

29

poem for jean

jean
i envy you the huge wind and the dust
the overpowering presence of all that sky
the enchiladas and tortillas
i envy you the warm springs and
clearwater ditch and
people who can be naked without looking skinned
i envy you sunset sandia towering
purple and surreal over desert and valley

jean
i envy you
though i love this place
the mist and the moist of it
the wet hot
the familiar with only a touch of the strange
but oh i miss the altogether strange of new mexico
i miss the mars
i miss the indian
the first growth which here is
layered over with abuse and regrowth

o water issuing from the rock of lama
o many coloured spring mountain flowers
o twisted pinyons and sagebrush

o green edged brown rio
o howling coyotes

o rainbow snow

o green   o brown   o purple

o dry

o azatlan

i miss you

Charlotte County, Virginia
July 1973

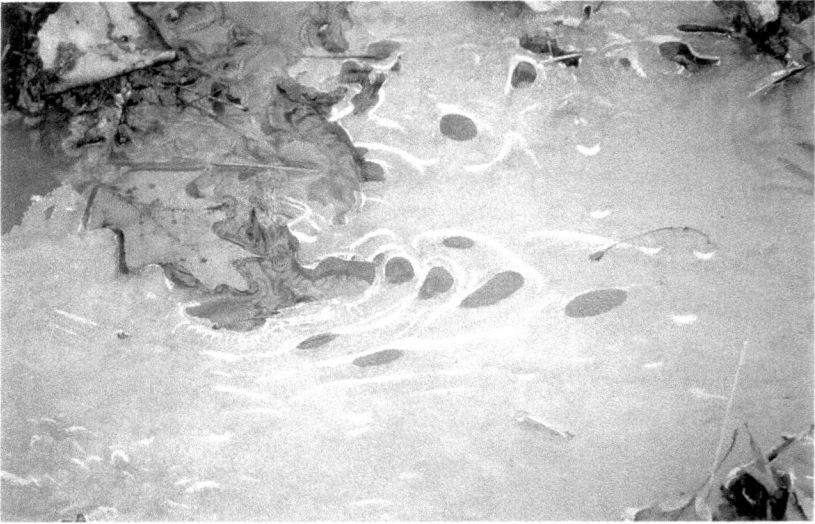

what to do?

in front of me are two pine trees
grown so close together that
they have assumed the shape of one tree.
no matter where they are placed
trees grow into a form of beauty.
growing through a grate in the city
they still become tree.

i think my neighbours mostly view them as
so many board feet of profit.
they think my meadow is wasted,
they offer to plough it up,
plant corn, wheat, soybeans.
they would give me a check,
and then the land would be used.

i think it is being used now,
returning some of the energy
that has been robbed from it.
i would like to have a cow,
some goats, maybe some chickens,
plant some vegetables and grain,
raise them with love.
well, maybe not very practical,
not something i've been very good at.
could i kill a chicken?
oh, god, i doubt it.

and now there's this.
busted.
more lawyers, more courts.
should we stay here?
should we sell the land
at a profit or a small loss?
go somewhere else?
run?
but where do we run to?
and once we've started running
where do we stop?

Charlotte County, Virginia
August 1973

fright

one night here in the garage
which is white-painted clapboard
falling to pieces on not-even cinder blocks
but assorted large rocks,
very dark on a moonless night,
pouring kerosene for the stove,
it was still cold,
i had the eery feeling of
the imminence of danger,
an overpowering fear of staying
and of course my rational
reluctance to leave followed
but i poured the kerosene,
recapped the container and left
with a sense of having escaped
in the nick of time

and of course nothing happened
but if i had stayed longer
i wonder
was it only a peculiarly adept
spider crouched in a web
that transfixed me in her stare?
or if i had stayed
was there real
danger?

Charlotte County, Virginia
1973

fish

green river flowing
high atop this space
of moss and fern bordered pools

quickened by darting shapes
that move from shadow to shadow
through flecks of sunlight
in universes six by three
edged at either end by the unknown

where earth squeezes sky
and creatures who move must
carry the sea
within walls of tissue

and green river flows
as current beneath
huge breakers of wind
that soothe and temper
the fiery extremes
of sun and dark

Charlotte County, Virginia
1973

flow

stream move
carry me move stream
carry me move carry me on
stream move
carry me
stream
water
flow over
me water flow
water carry me
seaward

Charlotte County, Virginia
1973

learning virginia

the darkly sensual soul of this place
emanates outward in
diminishing rays

moss-covered tangle of exposed shale,
half-lit under standing beech,
fallen timbers & climbing vines,
water rippling inch deep over
rocks & gravel, now seeming still in
misty pools broken
by darting shapes of life
whose five by three universe
encompasses all

as earlier i sat & felt
the hunger of the brook
along my lean thighs

it is a slower business
learning to love this place after
the extravagance of new mexico

Charlotte County, Virginia
October 1973

hail mary

hail mary, full of grace,
the lord is with you;

this is my catholic poem
my defiance to rome,
tinged still with apology;

this is to the embarrassment of the confessional
and the terror of hell,
to the image of woman as nun,
to frankincense,
to saint john's and saint mary's,
saint joseph's and saint mark's,
to stiff neck and sweaty underpants,
to god in the highest,
encapsulated in ancient formulae,
to painful erections and smothered guilt,
to a thousand years of suppressed books,
to truth burning on countless fires,

to my grandmother,
excessive as only a convert can be,
who gave me books about child saints,
scapulas to deliver me straight to heaven,

to saint anne, grandmother of god,
to saint joseph, his cuckold,
to bertrand russell,
infinitely more likable than child saints,
who made me a heathen at fourteen

to rome, imperial rome,
mother of power,
mistress of divided loyalty

holy mary, mother of god,
pray for us sinners,
now and at the hour of our death,
amen.

Charlotte County, Virginia
June 1973

metropolis

new york this trip
after passing through new jersey
which has every kind of noise
and commotion and progressive destruction
was sort of mellow and slow

the city doesn't change much anymore
except in the corporate strongholds
which get slicker and taller and
more tower of babel

for the rest it just lingers in its decay
a huge corroding warren of humanity

emilio's garden
is still a fine place for a drink

the new york times still tells it like it isn't
the air is still sinister with smoke and lack of trees
money in the pocket is still the only path out

around brooklyn bridge on the fdr drive
the smell of the sea is strong as ever
on the brooklyn side of the river
the watchtower's sign still bears witness
to its electrified jehovah

Manhattan
May 1973

backwater, megalopolis

lightless streets
leaky roofed barracks
television

in the next room
through the thin wall
our neighbour is
beating
his teenage son

he will cry
soft in his stiff bed
for us all

factory slum
heavy coal smoke
the rain
is our constant

Warminster, Pennsylvania
February 1973

41

south valley

genevieve
i miss the sun over your ammunition-crate house
the fierce southwest sun
on all those junked autos rusting back to earth

i miss the elm trees from my back window

the cottonwoods along the river, the russian olives

i miss the otters slipping from the bank
the swifts racing over the water
the ravens

i miss most knowing no one
having no past
making my name up as i went along

here, i miss myself

Warminster, Pennsylvania
winter 1973

christmas 1971

albuquerque this year
spent the twelve days of christmas
in an inversion

christmas day
we drove to jemez hot spring;
as ever we sunned and bathed
and smoked reefer
with congenial naked people,
chris took pictures of us with baby raven

but on our way there, from the mesa
a thick pall hung over the valley between
us & sandia

it seems somehow ominously
symbolic

South Valley
January 1972

valley poem

yesterday morning
elm filtered sun
speckled philodendron and carpet
with magic light of azatlan.

we bathed in clearwater ditch,
lay naked in warm pools of sun
beneath distant purple sandia

today
under rare steel
cottonwoods scattered themselves
upon the grassy verge of the rio.

now
the ravens sweep noisy circles
on wind breaking like ocean
around our walls

South Valley, New Mexico
October 1971

mescaline

is a natural trip with me.
        it is *natural* to me.
        i want to be outdoors, to be actively engaged —
        by ear, eye, (nose), touch,
                TOUCH   / temperature,
                          wet-dry
             Touch
        air-wind
            compounded of wet-dry
                    cold-warm
            mixed with sun

cold, damp, soggy,
            dry grass pressed into earth
                  against ass
dry grass under legs, with
    pimples of cold earth
            poking through

Touch,
of sound against ear —
the tremor of air set vibrating
by rocks & water

touch, touch, touch
why does it not

        come
           through

it is controlled, literary,
non-variable

let's try this instead:

45

i am
        relating
the movement of the water
    o   t   r
    v   h   o
        e   e   c
        r   k
                                s

to that
which registers
as sound
        against my ear

it is the only thing that i have done today.

Questa, New Mexico
November 1970

Photo courtesy of Christopher Barr. The author, at his portable typewriter in Albuquerque, ca. 1970.

november evening, questa

hypnotic in its grey web
the spider maw of television
feeds upon twelve captive eyes

through the frozen window moonlight
melts into an icy halo around
the green kerosene lamp,
beautiful in vain

the wandering jew, languishing for weeks
in a diminishing glass of water, sits
now in a flower pot between
television and moonlight,
sending forth new
green shoots

turned electric
the lamp could adorn
the artificial mantle of
a pretend fireplace somewhere
in new jersey or ohio or another
of the plastic-rose suburbs of purgatory

gretchen buys us packages of poison
disguised as instant cheese cake,
the lettuce at our table
also is poisoned
more subtly

at night we dream revolutions
instantaneous as nestle's quik

Questa, New Mexico
November 1970

48

Leaving Brooklyn, 1970

the back seat from the volkswagen
joined my growing-up comic books,
lots of science-fiction, 78 & 45 rpm records,
all stashed in a corner of my Mom's attic.

packed in the car was
everything we thought me might need
after cutting loose, Leary-like,
from our cultural moorings;

already adept at living out of the car
from the summer before,
cross-Canada camping,
we had the car reasonably organised:
the silverware had its appointed place
under the front passenger seat,
the insulated ice chest was behind
the same seat;
the Coleman stove had a tight spot
in the official luggage area
under the hood;
we had roof carriers
& up there we piled
pots & pans, other things
that would not mind rain
& being blown about.

we headed for New Mexico
because Ronald was there.
no plans beyond that.
certainly no plans to come back.
so long, New York.

oh, it wasn't really spur-of-the-moment.
we'd been a year talking;
Vancouver was our first thought
(speaking honestly, *my* first thought):
I always loved Canada.
but after our previous summer trip
I realised that
they did not necessarily love us.
(who could blame them?)

then there was a commune in Vermont
that we talked about for months..
it broke up before we got there,
but we drove up anyway;
it was the student strike time
& we hung out at Goddard,
a good place for contacts;
people told us about back-to-the-landers.
we had some NY $.
I was a union printer, Irene was temping for Kelly Girls,
we both made good money.
we lived by spending, but had a bit of cash in the bank,
buying land was not impossible.
talked to a 93-year-old farmer
who owned a valley & a mountain.
he was a great talker, no taciturn New Englander he,
told us how he'd gone to B.C. when he was young,
made some bread, came back & bought land.
Wanted to be sure you were going to farm,
not waste the land.

we talked to other people,
people who had been with the failed commune,
others who were still struggling
with the long winter,
the short growing season,

the cold.
the long, cold winter, came up all the time.
whole time we were there (it was May)
the sun hardly shone.

we realised it wasn't for us.
only way we could really do it was to get a loan,
then we'd owe money.
wages were low in Vermont, we'd work our asses off!
at least in New York we both made good money.
we had lots of illusions,
but behind it all, a bit of common sense.
we knew it just wouldn't work.

Ronald said come to New Mexico,
lots of hippies here,
stay with me, or camp in the national forest.

we took the two cats, too.
crazy idea.
the cats hated the car.
we did not even have cat carriers.
both cats ran away in Ohio.
Benny left first, in a state park.
we waited days, but he never came back.
the same day we gave up and left
Onda jumped out the window
in Macarthur, Ohio;
we tramped around the suburban neighbourhood
calling her name,
worried someone would call the cops
& report these two hippies
walking around their yard.

we could not find her.
Onda probably did okay,

she was a sweet cat,
probably found a home.
Benny less likely,
he was a paranoid freak of a cat.
losing the cats was not our best moment.
we felt bad, but
on the other hand,
once we reluctantly drove off
it felt like now we had really cut loose.

this is a good moment to change to the present tense:
late afternoon, crossing into Indiana
we decide to drop mescaline.
we stop in a grocery, buy beans & cheese for our dinner.

we are tripping as fireflies start in the fields.
we turn off onto a road in Indiana,
no idea where it goes:
one of those ideas that seem to make sense
when you are getting off on mescaline;
it becomes gravel, dirt,
goes on for miles into the country,
bordered by planted fields.

we stop & look at the fireflies.
the beans & cheese were a mistake:
I feel like my bowels want to explode.
I am in the field with my pants down,
trying to shit; Irene is shouting something,
there is a man coming towards us with a flashlight.
Irene shouts "hallo," but he does not answer.
it looks to me like he has a rifle in his other hand,
I am very scared, rush Irene into the car.
Irene thinks I saw menace where there was none:
I suspect she is right, but I am glad we left.

we turn around & go back to the highway,
stop at Ed's, the billboards have told us about it for miles:
the sign says "hippy beads," also "birdbaths."
out front are 50 cookie jars all identical.
we take a lid because it fits our lidless teapot.
It is getting chilly, I change from shorts
to long pants in the parking lot.

Route 50 again.
a wrong turn & we are on Route 41 south.
it is dark, we are in full trip,
a very disoriented trip.
I cannot imagine how to get back.
we are heading south, into *the South.*
paranoia.

finally I pull onto the shoulder.
I walk down the hill & try to shit.
there are big trucks racing by us;
I can see the vw shaking all over with each one,
other trucks are across the field;
we are between two highways,
squatted down I see them through
the high grass going to seed around me.
I am bewildered in mid-America,
en route without destination.
I cannot shit;
I feel like all America is trying
to pass through my bowels

I go back to the car & get Irene
& we sit & look at the fireflies.
days before we had set out
on a path in a wood in Ohio
with a stranger we met,
turned back as night started coming on

but lost the trail & we wandered
stumbling for hours in the dark woods;
where does man belong, I ask.
the other night in the woods we were out of place,
here we are bewildered, terrified.
we are back in the car.
I cannot understand the map.
Irene never understands maps.

a super highway truck stop.
we spend a long time in the car,
talking, touching each other.
we are inside the restaurant.
it is plastic.
hot chocolate & tea.

I am in the men's room,
still trying to shit America;
it is dingy & dank,
like Pennsylvania Railroad johns in New Jersey.

I am back at the table,
Irene leaves.
there are quite a few people.
they are all watching us. me.
my tea has white froth on top,
Maxwell House tea the tag says.
it is lukewarm, with the taste of dust.

we leave. the maps work now.
we must follow 41 through Evansville,
then catch 60 in Kentucky.
41 is incredibly bad.
every suburban discount store looms at us,
we stop & wash the windshield,
someone offers us help.

we drive on.
outside Evansville we pick up a farm boy.
I tell him how there are so many roads in Amerika,
how all you do is pick one & find
where it goes.
he does not respond.
I put the Iron Butterfly on the tape deck,
turn the volume all the way up.
the stereo speakers that used to be
in our living room in Brooklyn
are on either side of him.
it is doubtful whether In-a-Gadda-da-Vida penetrates.
when we let him out it is like a weight lifts from us.

we listen to c&w on the radio.
lug culture — some of the humour is good.
the Vice President says
something about drugs on the news.

we go on & on, pull over and look at the map,
decide on Kentucky Dam State Park.
we go fifteen miles out of our way to find it;
it is the first time we have
registered officially for camping.

we are camped next to a public lavatory;
as we pitch our tent
trains barrel through with a deafening roar;
the sun is rising.

On the road, mid-America
June 1970
Revisited March 2014

Easter 1970

3 a.m.
lights still on
they never go out now
protect us from the night
Electricity
and the terror of the skies
nineteen hundred and seventy years
since the ash of Hellenism
eddied around
the feet of the saviour

spring snow in New York and we
quietly inter Easter
our homage now
to the moon
alone
we sit amid the ashes
candles quickening upon our altars
and dance for the new shape
of our risen
god

Brooklyn
29 March 1970

Eternity

The sea persists in its ridiculous noise,
pretending to be immortal,
but actually minute by minute vanishing
into the air, changing

with the rivers and the rains, absorbing
and being absorbed. The crowds
on the beach, too, have their pretense
of immortality, but the greatest

of their monuments tumble into ruins,
outliving only their own
remembrance. The million creatures, land and sea,
live their lives and die.

But closest to eternality, reduced as much
as a thing can reduce,
infinite and indestructible in their tininess,
are the miles and miles of sand.

Manhattan
1969

Our Times

The dream of democracy,
imperfectly rendered from the garbled ruins of Athens,
has brought us here grovelling for hope in America;
the camps of the Roman armies
have sparked no wisdom with their fires,
and the legions of the Roman faith, reconfigured
by Constantine, have marched impotently splendid
through all the books that are our memory.
The keys of Byzantium were handed to the Turk,
but the line held at Vienna and the Pyrenees;
the tide reversed and Europe went on
to plunder America, enslave Africa, stumble into Asia.

The long bleeding retreat from world Empire began in Dublin,
as the focus of European conquest turned inward against itself;
the Habsburgs, no longer noble defenders,
bulwark of Christendom, petered out in Vienna,
and in Berlin the last Caesar retired into
belligerent irrelevance in Holland.
A generation later the battle was rejoined
and the whole fabric of civilisation seemed about to unravel.

So here we are with Europe divided and ineffective,
half prosperous, half enslaved,
all of us clinging to the shreds of memory
in this century where war became the true reality,
where infants cut their teeth on barbed wire
while their elders looked with bewilderment
on the wreckage of Europe and
the now ensnared hope of America.

Brooklyn
23 February 1969

On the Eve of Nixon

The slime-clogged Hudson
slips into the sewerage sea

> through the deltas of defiance
> gathered at the estuaries of America,
> thick with the coagulating blood
> of self-inflicted doom;

> already the turgid glacier of America,
> trapped these years between
> her encroaching seacoasts,
> grinds noisily forward, crushing,
> driving back toward resurrection,

the violet mountains of Manhattan
fade in the mists of Do,
an anachronism now,
the deathbed of senile rebellion,
a half-conscious prodigy
strangling in its own umbilical cord;
California will fall into the sea,
and the sated belly of glacial America
will ruminate upon its own satisfaction,
swallowing the half-continent in its gullet.
Obsolete as the Indian,
the rebels will stand in queues,

> waiting their bit part in a darkened theatre
> where the comedy has already failed;
> the first rebels and the last Tories
> of America, learning to play their part
> with the sullied streams and rotting forests,

with violet Manhattan,
with the ancient landlords of the Americas —
preserved and protected
to breed like the buffalo —

in safe numbers that cry
of the empty plains.

Manhattan
19 January 1969

night walk in the holy land

fifteen miles from nazareth
richard nixon crossed my path
i lifted my crucifix
but he removed his eyes
and rolled them in the dust

i allow your right to be he said
although i think it would be better were you dead
a convocation of rich men have sent me
and i will be well received
for there is no flaw in my credentials

his eyes were in my hands now
and i looked out
between my fingers

this path is unfamiliar i said
but i would hope that there is much
credential in our flaws
you will reach a point
where the light dims
and blinds you with its brightness;
take these your dusty eyes
and handed him the pebbles

Manhattan
1969

Dupont Circle / Everywhere

feel that cold on your back, baby
that's the cold breath of america
it bites like steel
STEEL HOT and STEEL COLD
that's america
cataracted eyes over
steel pistols, steel prisons
palsied hands
fumbling steel keys

rocky says *more guns*
what's good for south america
is good enough for newark
talk to america, nixon
tell it like it is, spiro
listen, CBS, tomorrow the big news
is YESTERDAY
riding firm in the saddle
on a blind mule

the BIG NEWS, the *big, big news*
is the silent majority of guns
that runs this country
the big news is mr & mrs america
humping in the dark
tight-lipped behind their mountain of guns

the big news is
they ain't never gonna come

Manhattan
1969

Dusk on Fifth Street

The mushroomed heat of the afternoon lingers
like smoke from a fired gun,
the breeze moves with heavy hot fingers
through the torpor of the trees

In the tenement courtyard two dogs tear
at a tattered piece of cloth
near to an aged cat asleep beneath a wicker chair,
drugged with the oppressive heat.

Hardly a figure moves in the windows opposite;
behind me the room is still —
the record has finished, but no one changes it,
and the throaty hum of the speakers

pervades the room like the voice of the humid dusk.
Skyscraper lights pierce
the haze that clings like a dry husk
about the ripened city,

a lone shaft of scarlet streaks the sky
as the vast, gathering darkness
broods above its prey, then, with a soundless sigh,
settles upon the city.

Manhattan
July 1968

Reverie

Under the lilac on the lawn, I slept
with Athens and with Carthage,
as the long shadows of the afternoon leapt
across my face

to stir my dream's awakening,
till I was young with time,
and, older than man's christening,
I saw the vast enigma

of life unfold and fold in again
like some reluctant flower
that feels the threatening rain
and regrets the sun

Manhattan
1968

Suburban Roadhouse

Lord, the misery of life
the long, devastating loneliness
of this woman across the bar from me
playing with the orange in her wiskey sour
happiness haunts her face like a shadow
of which she cannot find the substance

Lord, why have you given me such eyes
I cannot bear to look so deep into people

man, woman
loveliness, light,
transcendance, glory,
foresakenness
I shall go mad
I shall vomit my sickened soul upon the world
I shall drink hemlock again and again and live

If I only I had hands that could touch

New Jersey
1968

65

The Scent of Lilac

Not quite so lovely nor so lasting
as this scent of lilac on the breeze,
and with never quite the gathering strength
of a river embracing the seas,

but real and strong and quick with hope
and all that mattered for a day or two
in weeks and weeks of pain —
your love was all that I knew I knew

and all that I wanted to know.
A green mist hovers now among the trees:
I must content myself with that
and the lilac-tainted breeze.

Manhattan
June 1968

A Certain Slant

I have known summer days in the country
   that were as lovely as you;
and I have known music and poetry
   to be more true,

more real, than any love you own.
   And if, at the moment, I wonder how,
no doubt I shall learn to live alone,
   and wonder at now.

So let us say that it was only sex,
   be friends again instead,
pretend that what we have shared
   was only a bed.

But not easily shall I forget a certain slant
   of morning light on your shoulder;
and not for a long time will the warmth of a woman
   make me anything but colder.

Manhattan
May 1968

Adrift in Jamestown

If I could make of this tangle
of loves and needs some pattern,
or if I could trace down
one thread to its source;

if I could see not only the trees
but the grain of the wood
and the breath of the leaves
and the flow of the sap;

if I knew why a touch
of the hand can move the mind
or a whisper of thought
move the hand;

if I could understand all or much
or even one thing, then I might
live as I must live.

But here I am:
thought without body,
hand without mind,
eyes deaf,
ears blind.

Jamestown, New York
March 1968

Elizabeth Street

The pines pillage my memory
with their sighing,
I cannot understand nor explain
my ancient crying.

At three in the afternoon
bedraggled dawn filters
weakly down five storeys
through dirty windows.

Somewhere in the world
radiators rattle,
an electric motor cycles,
coffee perks.

All this I understand.
It is real
I touch the table's top:
it is hard.

But I cannot understand nor explain
this ancient crying
nor how the pines pillage my memory
with their sighing.

Manhattan
1968

Lament for Loneliness

How many lovely lonelinesses
have I known —
by unfrequented lakes
and unfashionable beaches,
along brooks that hide in deep woods,
on wind-chafed summits
and in lonely corners of populous deserts;
along the coast of Nova Scotia
and the flat beaches of Delaware,
on Mt. Scott at night
and in the cedar swamps of south Jersey —
and when I think of the world they are making
where there will be no loneliness —
where people see lists of the things they may not do —
No Swimming, No Walking, No Standing, No Dancing,
No This, No That —
I do not know whether to cry for what they are doing
or to laugh because they think it can be done.

Manhattan
July 1968

Refuge

When the snow has ceased and the rain beats
incessant upon the roof —
for never now will we know end of this long precipitation —
then cling,
cling fast to me,
and as the water creeps over the door sills and across the floors
give me once again
this momentary release,
the only fulfilment we have known,
our animal consolation
while the world bleeds slowly to death.

Do not bother me
with the system builders and the dreamers,
the saints and the philosophers:
let them rot in their graves.

This little tent of light and safety
is our only refuge
amidst the encroaching darkness;
for outside is only an endless falling of cold rain
upon a desolate shore.

Manhattan
1968

Thoughts at Coney Island

The beaches already begin to resemble their close
summer patchwork quilt of humanity,
the seams bound by the bulletins and analyses
blared from transistor radios.

John Kennedy, Martin Luther King,
and a multitude fallen
in our foreign and in our domestic war
lie in their graves.

In the City of the Angels Robert Kennedy waits,
senseless of the alien chunk of metal
lodged in his brain.

The next president of the United States will be
another choice of nobody,
another master by accident.

I look around me and I see a theatre in flames,
the audience drugged and sleepy,
hypnotised by the puppet lifting his arms to flail the air
in his laughing dance of death.

Coney Island
May 1968

Drumbeat

I know the beat of this drum,
       I can feel its message roll,
but my mind is blank, and my lips are dumb
       for the drummer's music
is a tongue forgotten, his message is all
       unknown. Outward and upward,
pounding my ears, the drumbeats fall
       again and again and again.

Manhattan
1968

73

Ready to Go

A paper valise and a green chemise
with a pint of tea and a cup of stone
        are enough to bluff
                any old fool.

So what if I mumble and what if I stumble
with a pint of tea and a cup of stone
        I'll deliver a quiver
                to any old breast.

Of course in my ageing I'm often raging
with a pint of tea and a cup of stone
        but satisfied is gratified
                and I get by.

Manhattan
1967

Unmasked

Someday, when the nylon threads are cut
and the pattern is complete
in the frayed edges of our synthesis,

our eyes will walk no longer masked
down the corridors of darkness
teeming with our emptiness.

I don't care:
the meaning's there.

(Could it be
that the world is free,
that everyone knows
how the spirit grows
when the child in the tomb
remembers the womb?)

Couldn't be.
Take tea.

Visions will not save us, nor visions.
It is chemistry that slays us,
and there is no redress.

New Jersey
1967

Short List

Yes. I number this
(the hard patter of rain)
among the things I shall miss.
This — and the long sigh
of the night wind.
(I do not know why.)

But love, too, ends.
And I shall miss most
the rising, falling,
many-levelled voices of friends.

New Jersey
1967

This Poet's New Philosophy

If that is what they want
from me then I too ca
n make a poem in
the shape of
a triang
le, s
ee?

or
I even
can turn i
t upside down-
-I will confess th
at it seems silly to m
e, but if they want it, ok

aw
shit
!

Manhattan
1967

The Wind

Lay your leaves on the wind, willow,
      for the wind goes on
long after this restless whispering
      in your leaves has ceased,
long, long after all the whispering
        in the world has ceased
        and only the cold whine
        of the ancient wind
        upon the weathered rock
        relieves the long silence
        of a dead planet.

        The wind, the wind
  on a thousand youthful worlds
        rushes across the land,
        steeped in the momentum
        of the life-giving seas.

The ancient, whispered tale resounds,
        strange and lovely, lonely —
        incomprehensible with grief,
        wild with inexpressible joy;
        young as life itself,
    as the new buds on the green shoot,
    old as the gnarled and twisted vine
    that long ago shed its final vintage;
young with the persistence of the struggling roots
        in the resisting rock.

Lay your leaves on the wind, willow,
      for the wind goes on,
      the wind, the wind,
      the wind goes on.

Huntsville, Alabama, 1966

78

Succession

Still, across the lake,
the golden sunbeams flake
upon the leaves, gently rustling;
the trees behind us fling
their long shadows halfway
to the other shore: the day
is in its final throes,
the racing pulse slows,
and softly, without a sound,
the night creeps upward from the ground.

The full moon sweeps
the lake; a bullfrog leaps
into the water; the whippoorwill
calls — the air is still

with a stillness not of sound;
dark shadows linger round
the base of every tree.

The breeze lifts, the branches stir gently;
a thick veil passes between earth and skies;
lightning flashes, quickly dies;
soft rain patters high amongst the leaves
then batters and rages, cleaves
its way to the earth below.

Suddenly the rains slow;
the brook babbles loudly in the night;
the moon emerges, fiercely white.

Barely at first, the night pales:
one by one each star fails.
The birds, in one great rush,
break the morning hush;
a thin mist hovers above the lake;
footfalls break,
treading the cold sand
that rims the edge of lake and land.

The darkness fades in the west;
the sun emerges from the stagnant forest
and glimmers off the slippery wetness
of the rocks; the sun presses
ever onward across the world:
relentlessly the brilliant day's unfurled.

Fort Sill, Oklahoma
1966

Cameron Hotel

Yesterday morning
the spring sun beamed and the myrtle bloomed
amidst the cast-off dregs of last year's spring;
the blue sky lay shattered upon the windswept lake;
from the high oak the rope swung back and forth
as though remembering the years and years of boys
who had plunged themselves into the lake.

The derelict gardens were marked only here and there
by the pale shadow of an ordered plan;
the ancient privet rows,
long remiss from their intended trimness,
fought their way upward through the sea-like shade
that had overtaken them;
on the wizened apple waited another year's hopeful buds.

Weathered and old,
the house stood nobly upon the high bluff,
the nightly victim of destructive juvenility's
smoking and drinking parties amongst its forsaken rooms,
surrounded by the evidence of its own abandonment —
the furniture, the plumbing, the very mattresses from its beds
lay strewn beneath its windows
as though some vast intestinal disturbance
had spewn forth the contents of its interior.

The wind moved freely through the shattered windows
and the light fluttered across the rain-streaked floors,
but the house maintained its long silence,
the sole guardian of its forgotten past.
Aware, perhaps, that for the last time were its weathered,
paintless clapboards soaking up the spring sun —

that the trees would come in leaf
and the rain would fall
and the sun would flicker and dance
above only an empty space in the wood.

Remembering, perhaps, the moment
when a man had stood upon this site
and decided that here he would build a house;
remembering the ceaseless summer whisper
of the trees above its rooftop,
or the long succession of voices
that had moved along its corridors,
or the quiet brook that once rippled through the wood
or the gleaming, man-made lake that had engulfed it.

Sifting its memories, perhaps —
forgetting the long degradation
that had moved it from inn to speakeasy to inn again,
but inn of convenience
whose roomers seldom stayed the night,
and finally to emptiness,
forgetting the bare brown of its clapboards
and the peeling paint of its walls;
wanting again the laughter and gayety of life
rushing through its halls like wine,
remembering its noble service as a waystation
on the underground railroad to freedom in Canada.

A part of the past, dreaming of the past,
the old house approached the end of the day,
and with night felt the inexorable flames
creeping up its dried timbers,

until the gallons and gallons of water thrown upon it
could barely save the surrounding wood,
and the next day, brown and sooty,
still trickled down the hill and into the lake.

The house burnt furiously on
all through the night —
disdainful of the watching crowd
and the ineffective fire engines;
disdainful of the world which had forgotten,
a world which would only have done with the wrecker's boom
what the fire did so much more splendidly.

Disdainful —
of a world which no longer mattered.

Fort Sill, Oklahoma
1966

Fire in the Hole!

The gulls rise and drop;
the tall grass bends to touch the sand;
the wind is heady with the sea.
Wave after wave breaks upon the shore,
but in the distance the sea ripples peacefully
and not a whitecap shows upon the vast expanse of water.
The world in its ancient order is unconcerned
with the bits of steel and wood that bob upon the waves.
Unconcerned
with all man's fiery accomplishment locked in their vitals
like flaming arrows in a tight bow.
Fire in the hole! Fire in the hole! Fire in the hole!

Across the frozen northland
the dormant line of fire stretches;
a flock of ducks sweeps south,
unmindful of their sudden strategic power —
relays click, the planes go out,
pregnant with destruction;
the fate of the planet teeters in the balance.
Fire in the hole! Fire in the hole! Fire in the hole!

Somewhere in Asia an obscure tyrant provokes a neighbour;
a ripple of fear passes through the world's capitals;
a hundred ancient cities sleep in imminent danger.
But the pelican is not moved from his search;
the captive fish is aware only of the swooping death
which has enveloped him;
the pelican knows only the quiet gnawing of his own hunger.
Fire in the hole! Fire in the hole! Fire in the hole!

The seas have not changed their inevitable cadence
through all man's eventful stay upon his world;
the grass has not forsaken its long struggle
with the unstable sand;
the same cool wind soothes the same hot brow —
but the heat is from within,
day by day it grows,
a fever racing out of hand.
Fire in the hole! Fire in the hole! Fire in the hole!

Fort Sill, Oklahoma
summer 1966

Requiescat for Man

We are lost, my father,
we are lost, my son,
we are lost at last,
and the long tale done.

We have taken our playthings,
our little toys,
and knocked down the world
with a great big noise.

Fort Sill, Oklahoma
1966

Military Poem

What match ever in calm again
the morning peace of after rain
when gentle breeze softly caressed
shivering leaves, water-dressed?
What ever again soothe the eyes
like steaming lake wearing muddy skies?
Where ever again the quiet thrill
of rushing brook's rippling trill?

Others perhaps in the city can see
the inner calm to make them free.
For me the brook in its concrete walls
is all that speaks as evening falls:
trapped and dirty, clogged with slime,
the sullied brook flows and cries to me
of the passing world and the boundless sea.

Fort Sill, Oklahoma
1966

On A Petunia Growing at the Edge of the Wood

Poor, transplanted offspring of the tropic sun,
by what thoughtless gardener
cast aside with last autumn's leaves
to grow all summer
and face the unexpected autumn of the north —
How you've flourished here
unaware that the summer sun
was not that of far Brazil.
Now, struggling to clamber above
the discarded foliage of the decidous summer,
do you suspect that the frigid temper
of the nights will not abate?
That soon above the deep-piled leaves
more deep will pile the snow?

The giants all about you sleep
secure in the rhythm of an unfamiliar world;
but you, condemned by the inevitable turning of the earth,
will sink into an endless winter.

Yet, come the spring,
one of your countless seeds
may spring to life
and hold once more those crimson trumpets
above the warm earth that once again
will grow so unexpectedly cold.

New Jersey
autumn 1966

Never

The skies are clear and the stars are bright,
the wind is soft, it does not moan;
the pines are still in the wood tonight:
they do not sigh, I sigh alone.

The water ripples with the same light sound,
the fire burns in the grate;
the spring of morning is tightly wound,
the hour grows more late.

Soon sprung, the gathering day will rush
across the glistening land.
But never your voice will break the hush
nor hand lay hold my hand.

Fort Sill, Oklahoma
1966

The Other Shore

I saw the sea on another shore,
I dreamt that sea, I dreamt much more;
I dreamt that the world was changed and new,
I dreamt much more: I dreamt of you.

I dreamt the wind upon my flesh,
the spray-filled air like silver mesh;
I dreamt that love outlasted time
in more than word, in more than rhyme.

I dreamt the sun in a cloudless sky,
the salt-tinged air, the seagull's cry;
I dreamt our love still strong, still true,
enduring yet, not death-pierced through.

I dreamt your eyes, alive with light,
defying sleep and endless night;
I dreamt — and in the night forgot
your changeless, mute, eternal lot.

The wit that will not flash again,
the flesh that will not feel the rain,
the tender hand whose trembling clutch
will never feel my answering touch,

the eyes that once could light a room,
that now are steeped in ageless gloom,
flashed last night, gleamed with fire,
lit my dreams with old desire.

The night grew pale, turned to day,
swept the dream-filled night away.
And the morning breeze, and the bright fair sky,
burnt my lungs and stung my eye.

Fort Sill, Oklahoma
1966

Farewell

Sleep well, my love.
This night is long enough,
and deep, to give you rest.
It clasps about you like a silken cloak
in whose enormous folds to sink,
forever unaware.

This night supplants all earthly care;
Be not disturbed, though hours waste,
the clocks have stopped within your breast,
and nothing else will last so long
as till the morning break again.

What's now untold you'll never tell;
you've seen the first and last of wrong.
Sleep well, my love, sleep well,
for more than this there will not be;
Sleep well through all eternity.

Fort Sill, Oklahoma
1966

Transfiguration

Above the line of trees
on the other side
the dawn is about to break;
but is dawn a matter of sun cresting the horizon
or mind perceiving it as such?
Would a fox from the woods
stop and watch the sun rising?
Would he know it was dawn
with no words to name it?

Does it matter?

In the cloudless sky
the half-risen orb of the sun
now sparkles on the water,
and in stark contrast
against its light,
veiled in mist,
I see a boy arise naked
from the steaming pond of evening.

Beads of darkness
evaporate from his flesh.
His pale body is tightened, tense,
sunlight flashing along wet loins and chest,
as he turns and stares into the sun,
lifts his arms in silent supplication,
and sublimes
into a clear mist.

New Jersey
1965, revisited August 2014

On My Dog Lying in the Sun

In the April sun
how soft and warm
your ripply fur gleams;
and from your tranquil eyes
reflects no awareness
that someday the sun will not shine so warm
nor the breeze rustle so softly through your fur.

You linger in an everlasting present
where every night has its morning,
where no terror outlives its moment,
all unaware of the vast gulf beneath you.

Unaware.
Except of the warm sun
and the rustling wind
and the morning that never fails to come.

New Jersey
1965

94

March

The first, desperate breath of summer
tinged the air this afternoon;
the spring rain had ceased and partly settled
into the depths of the lake.
How clear, crystal, the surface was, and,
a few feet below, the sun held
by the brown muddiness suspended in the water.

How I longed to strip and swim across,
and find the leafing woods again,
the whole lake enclosed in its shell of silence,
the houses gone,
the cars,
the new highway bridge.

I will come back and feel the cool caress of your waters again,
tonight,
when the windows are shuttered with darkness,
and across the lake
the deep forest of the night
cloaks the water's edge.

New Jersey
March 1965

View from a High Place

Since the dawn the wind's been rising,
rushing from the west, cold and clear.
It is good to be alone here, to feel the cold sting
against my flesh, to hear

the wind howl and moan about these heights;
to watch the day upon the run
across the chequered plain, the scattered lights
of farms come on, one by one;

I see the night obscure the land, every spark
become as lone and separate as each star overhead.
Islands all: islands in the encroaching dark.
To each farm the germ of light is fed

through unseen, narrow corridors. Who knows
what other links elude our sight?
Through what great circuit power flows
to feed the stars their blazing light?

Sussex County, New Jersey
1965

Blackberries

In the summer we would walk among the fields,
picking blackberries along the way,
dreaming in the blistery sun.
I remember in the midst of January
how summer's memories lingered
around a jar of blackberry jam.
Thorns in the fingers, scratches on the arms,
hands purple with ripeness,
stems to be plucked,
berries crushed and cooked,
the purple foam bubbling on top,
then poured into jars, sealed with the puzzling wax,
clouds gathering in soft paraffin
like a wispy veil above a dark sea.

What now of the blackberry?
Is all that same black lusciousness
of sun and rain and dusty earth
so neatly packed in air-tight jars
on clean-swept supermarket shelves?

What do *they* know of the blackberry?
Do *they* know
without sugar added how sweet enough
was the tender-thorned dewberry on a summer day?
Do *they* know the whet that makes the feast?
That blackberries should be eaten out of the hand
on the way home from leaps into the lake?
How cool enough were the berries, hot from the summer sun?
How they soothed,
slithering down parched throats, seeds and all.
No seeds between *their* teeth,
and *they* think *they* know the blackberry.

Gone the accidental fields, spared from development
through the years of the war and the immediate post-war;
gone with them the blackberries;
the summer remains, and the sun,
shining on black macadam,
on gridiron streets and gridiron minds.
No bare feet against this soil now,
no long dreams in the summer sun,
no boy's flesh warms this cold lake,
no paths lead through these fenced-in yards.

And what has this too-perfect jam to do
with the blackberry's haunted tale
of a whole summer's hoarded wealth?
the lake rippling beneath darkened skies,
the naked skin towelled by the rising wind of a sudden storm,
the lightning's flash above the swaying fields,
bent to the line of houses stark,
flushed into orange-red by a beam of sunlight
breaching the dark clouds,
the sticker's tugging at one's trouser legs.
And then the sun returning to the cave-dark skies,
the gem-like beads on the rain-wet leaves.

Jam was good enough for winter,
but who wanted jam
when the hot cloak of summer stifled the land,
when fresh from the icebox,
sprinkled with sugar and bathed in cream,
cool as an April swim,
came the ripe soul of summer itself.

New Jersey
1965

98

Legacy

Dream of stars, if dream you must,
     for stars will not be held.
Mix not your dreams with earthly dust
     lest they be easily felled.

The peaks that we can not sustain
     are all that matter afterward.
When all is shattered these remain;
     the mastered stone, the well-wrought word.

New Jersey
1965

Spring 1965

Summer's blowing in, fast upon December's cold;
the sodden earth trembles underfoot,
its icy exoskeleton loosing hold,
vanishing like long-descended soot
from summer fires: merged into the fertile soil,
returning in the cycle whence it came.
The sullen, lifeless hills make foil
to vaunt the brilliant, waxing flame
that shortly warmed the southern seas,
that blazed upon the Argentine,
that now brings sap uprushing through the trees
amongst these northern woods; unseen,
foregathering strength, the summer waits within
to garb the hills in soft green mist;
the sway of night grows every day more thin;
winter flees to keep its yearly tryst
with southern lands. But here the warm winds blow
again; the earth casts off its long disease;
the brooks flash, and the lakes glow,
the dark rivers rush to the gleaming seas.

New Jersey
1965

Snow Sonnet

The snow from yesterday's storm
dances and plays upon the wind,
twisting and whirling without form,
rising, falling on the lake's icy rind.
The great, footless plain stretches away
beneath the sombre, lowering sky;
nothing moves, nothing's moved all day
except the wind from the west, cold and dry,
and the icy boughs that twist and rage.
Deep in the earth the roots hoard
their precious summer's wage;
imperceptibly the earth moves toward
the never-failing turning of the tide:
the unkindled flame waits inside.

New Jersey
1965

Equipoise

Upon the lake the moonbeams lie,
quicksilver filaments of the vaulted sky,
upon whose spangled vastness night
trembles by some fearsome sleight.

Fragile as the rippling waves
on whose backs the moon engraves
softly-pulsing silver veins
is the balance which restrains
universe from caving in,
cloven like a rusty tin,
trampled underfoot and left,
unbeknowing, unbereft.

New Jersey
1965

Thirst

Frantic in the wind the willows
seem to whisper
that the summer knows
no path except through winter;
that the leaves must die
before the soil's renewed;
that beneath the uncomprehending sky
it does no good to sit and brood
upon the aimlessness of life;
that if this short span is filled
with hopeless fear and aimless strife,
yet for a moment when the clatter's stilled
and the sun sparkles across the sheer lake
on the breathless wind of autumn —
then suddenly a thirst no draught can slake
fills us and strikes us dumb —
a thirst more marvellous than any taste
that ever thrilled the subtlest palate;
and what seemed life's hopelessness, life's waste
is nothing — is less than last year's sweat
upon a corpse's brow —
and thirst alone has meaning now.

Fate, bring on your fearsome whips,
seal with death these breathing lips,
but *this* is ours, our gift of breed,
this, our own insatiable need:
Quenched we are, though quenchless cursed,
drenched in our all-conquering thirst;
Come, come and do your worst,
but *this* is ours, this endless thirst.

New Jersey, 1965

103

Lament for Two Worlds

Harness the oceans,
tame the night wind.
Let no wild storms
outrage man's mastery
of his planet.

Build a new world.
Forget the old.
Forget that long progression
from the steaming swamps;
forget that half man's life
lies hidden from himself.

Forget.
And bury deep the forgotten past —
lest suddenly some day,
when the fierce sun blazes upon a steel world,
for half a moment a whisper of rustling leaves may come
from the deep, hidden chambers of the inner ear;
the seas may sound, crescendo-like,
on the dark shores of the mind

and all in a rush
man's mighty edifice of steel and brick
will crash to the earth like a shattered drum
and deep, deep within
will rise the desperate certainty
that never —
never —
will there be
a world so lovely, tamed,
as once was this one, wild.

New Jersey, 1965

104

September Wind

Joy is the world! Joy that's in me,
whispering, whispering: Ecstasy
waits beyond the furthest hill —
Wait no more at the window sill,
race with the wind and the breathless sun!
Life's a race not to be won,
but race regardless beneath the trees,
race with the restless, aching breeze

New Jersey
1965

Hope

If men were Gods, and Gods were free
then hope would spring eternally,
but men are men, and gods are slaves,
and hope's interred in dusty graves.

New Jersey
1965

Enchantment

The spray's become a silvery mesh
stretched above the strand,
the wind's turned cool against the flesh,
the heat's gone from the sand.
It seems I briefly closed my eyes
and magic night's been wrought.
Awaking to these changeling skies,
has all been as it ought?
Were my eyes shut an age or two?
Or was it but an hour?
And was it dreamt or was it true
that, moved by some dark power,
great nations rose and after fell,
while here I lay beneath this spell.

New Jersey
1964

Unknowing

When earth of living green is shorn,
its central fires all grown cold,
its ancient surface smooth and worn,
and not a peak, nor even wold,
remains upon its face —
then, still, across the airless night,
the stars will take their place.
Unwinking, fierce will shine their light
upon the barren sphere,
and none will know, nor any care,
how much lies buried here.

New Jersey
1964

Linger

Hear the wind. It whispers softly
        through the rippling fields of hay.
Hear it calling, calling darkly,
        come away, come away.

See the evening pressing heavily
        on the quickly-fleeing day,
gleaming yet beyond the willow,
        far away, far away.

Let me linger at the window
        and catch each dying ray,
for when gently breaks the morrow
        I'll be so far away.

New Jersey
1964

South Street Station

Across the track, against the night,
so gently slipping past the light,
the silent stream of falling flakes,
a soft-edged world of whiteness makes.
The cushioned wind that softly moans
fills the sagging roof-line's slack,
smoothes the sunken cobblestones,
gains upon the stairway's black.
Fall snow, fall, pile deep, pile deep,
drift about our earthbound feet;
forever let the soft wind creep
its twisty path through earth's cold sheet;
forever let this gentle snow
mask the naked light-bulb's glow.

Newark, New Jersey
1964

110

Testament of a Forgotten Army

It may be the sun shone as ever and the skies were fair —
but our lives were bound
to the tormented soil beneath our feet;
we had not strength to stare
too long upward; our eyes were fastened to the ground;
only when the skies let loose upon us
with rain, or weighed us down with heavy sleet,
did they intrude upon our consciousness.

Ours it was to make our way without fuss
across the mournful earth;
to nourish the soil with precious blood
and lie at last in a field without a name.
Such was our mission, no more, no less;
it brought us no great fame,
required no great skill,
only the patience to plod through the mud
where once wild roses crept.
But, oh, my God, how long we've lain,
how long we've lain unwept.

Say of us what you will:
We did what we could,
lived while we had to,
upheld a cause we never understood,
died at last without protest.
For long we held the line,
though they were many and we were few,
and if at the last we broke and fled to the west,
we did not lie still
as they marched across our backs,
we fought with all the strength we had to fight,
but they flowed through our lines like molten wax;

before their hordes we turned in flight
and went where we were swept.
And, oh, my God, how long we've lain,
how long we've lain unwept.

The meadows have long been green again
and bright each year with springtime flowers;
the damage we wrought at such great cost
has been healed by the wind and the rain.
The battle and the war together were lost,
and the world has forgotten that ever we fell.
For we left no glories to keep us in mind,
no victories of which to tell;
only our widows we left behind
to bear sons that were not ours;
we are not aware that the earth is cold,
our sleep is too deep, and our memories too old.
But, oh, my God, how long we've lain.
How long we've lain unwept.

New Jersey
1964

In Spite of Donne

Every man is an island, in spite of Donne:
adrift alone in a vast sea
with only the casual touch
of a passing hand
to make bearable his long estrangement.
But the hand slips, and the mind reels, for no clutch
is strong enough to hold this one
hand against the force of faceless time
or make be that which would not be.

Poor, fluttery breath
when last expelled will not be reinstalled;
and we who breathe on
have no recourse except to strive higher while yet we may
and wait until the far horizon's palled
and all is swept before the storm's force.

Through the long night the seas will rise
and when the day breaks no light
will breach the skies.
But the seas will reach in vain to where
we have already made good our escape:
drowned in the sea of our own despair.

New Jersey
1964

113

Seeds

the soft, furry seeds of the willow
cling to the folds of my jacket;
I cannot greatly care
about all mankind's crises and discontents,
so long as the willow tosses its seeds
and the soft wind lays them
on the waiting earth.

New Jersey
1964

114

Another Year

Beneath this sheet of spotless white
sleeps all summer's heat tonight.
Rest content and never fear:
comes at last another year.

The ice will melt, the rivers flow;
trees may die, but new seeds grow.
Nothing's lost but is regained:
All must wax that once has waned.

Though dying eyes may find it dim,
dawn will burst above the rim,
new life come where old has passed,
nothing change, nothing last.

New Jersey
1964

ABOUT THE AUTHOR

Robin Matthews grew up in rural New Jersey. Trained as a printing press operator, he was drafted into the U.S. Army during the Viet Nam War. Following his discharge, he moved to Manhattan and co-founded the poetry magazine *Sanskaras* with Ronald Hobbs. Matthews left the east coast and mainstream America in 1970 to start a family and pursue an alternative lifestyle in New Mexico. During this period, his poetry and prose were published in several, mainly underground, publications. Later he studied creative writing at Goddard College, and then returned to work and residence in the southeast. Matthews is now retired from his second career as a computer programmer, and lives on a farm in Virginia.

www.ingramcontent.com/pod-product-compliance
Lightning Source LLC
Chambersburg PA
CBHW051734090426
42738CB00010B/2255